GREAT MINDS OF SCIENCE

Johannes Kepler

Discovering the Laws of Planetary Motion

Mary Gow

Enslow Publishers, Inc.

40 Industrial Road   PO Box 38
Box 398   Aldershot
Berkeley Heights, NJ 07922   Hants GU12 6BP
USA   UK

http://www.enslow.com

The author appreciates the support of the Andrew W. Mellon Foundation Travel Fellowship Program, which made it possible for her to do research for this book at the History of Science Collections at the University of Oklahoma.

Library of Congress Cataloging-in-Publication Data

Gow, Mary.
     Johannes Kepler : discovering the laws of planetary motion / Mary Gow.
        p. cm. — (Great minds of science)
     Summary: A biography of Johannes Kepler, the astronomer and mathematician who formulated the three laws of planetary motion.
     Includes bibliographical references and index.
     ISBN 0-7660-2098-3
     1. Kepler, Johannes, 1571–1630—Juvenile literature. 2. Astronomers—Germany—Biography—Juvenile literature. [1. Kepler, Johannes, 1571–1630. 2. Astronomers.] I. Title. II. Series.
     QB36.K4 G69   2003
     520'.92—dc21
                                                            2002014588

Printed in the United States of America

10 9 8 7 6 5 4 3 2 1

To Our Readers:
We have done our best to make sure all Internet Addresses in this book were active and appropriate when we went to press. However, the author and the publisher have no control over and assume no liability for the material available on those Internet sites or on other Web sites they may link to. Any comments or suggestions can be sent by e-mail to comments@enslow.com or to the address on the back cover.

Contents

1 The Plan of the Universe 5

2 Childhood 13

3 Discovering Copernicus 25

4 Solids and Spheres 36

5 Turmoil and Tycho 49

6 Two Laws of
Planetary Motion 60

7 Snowflakes, Galileo,
and Prague 73

8 Brides, Barrels, and Witches 81

9 Harmony and
   the Third Law 91

10 Final Years 99

   Activities 109

   Chronology 115

   Chapter Notes 118

   Glossary 124

   Further Reading
   and Internet Addresses 126

   Index 127

The Plan of the Universe

"SPEED LIMIT 17,500," READS A YELLOW sign posted in the International Space Station. Astronauts from countries around the world float past the sign as they travel between laboratories and living modules. On board the Space Station, astronauts conduct scientific experiments and research new technologies. They aim telescopes at stars in our galaxy and beyond. As the astronauts work, eat, and sleep, the Space Station is always moving. About 220 miles above us, it constantly circles Earth. Traveling at 17,500 miles per hour, the Space Station orbits our planet every 92 minutes.

When the Space Station was planned, scientists calculated exactly how fast it needed to travel in order to stay in orbit. The calculations they did were based on natural laws. These natural laws explain the relationships between objects in space. They govern the movements of planets, moons, and stars. The man who discovered three of these laws was a visionary mathematician who lived 400 years ago. His name was Johannes Kepler.

Johannes Kepler had "an almost unbelievable desire to learn the causes of things."[1] The universe, he believed, had a kind of mathematical beauty. Kepler was certain that there were mathematical explanations for the movements of all the planets and their arrangement in space—a plan of the universe. His goal in life was to figure out this plan. This led Kepler to many groundbreaking discoveries.

As Kepler sought this plan of the universe, he constantly asked questions. He doggedly pursued answers. As a result, he gave the world a new, more accurate model of the solar system. Kepler's work revealed the planets' true paths

Astronauts Mark Shuttleworth, Yury Onufrienko, and Roberto Vittori (left to right) under the speed limit signs in the International Space Station on April 27, 2002. Note that the speed is given as 17,500 miles per hour and also as 28,000 kilometers per hour.

through space. It also showed the distances between the planets and the laws that explain their movements.

Throughout his life, Kepler faced many challenges. Sickness and family difficulties marred his childhood. He lived in a time of religious and political change in Europe. Several times, when rulers changed, he had to move to another city in order to freely practice his religion. Money was also a constant worry for Kepler. Even when he was Imperial Mathematician of the Holy Roman Empire, his salary was seldom fully paid. At one time, Kepler's mother was accused of being a witch. For fourteen months, she was held in prison, not knowing if she would be tortured or even burned at the stake.

Kepler's life was not all misery, however. Good fortune, some happiness, and great success graced his life. His noble character won him many friendships. He married twice and had several children. Kepler also received a fine education, during which he found the two passions of his life: religion and astronomy. Over the course of his life, Kepler's quest to understand the universe gave him great pleasure. When he found the answer to a difficult problem, he was delighted.

"Man's soul," Kepler wrote, "is kept alive, enriched, and grows by that thing called knowledge."[2] The pursuit of knowledge was Kepler's greatest joy. Enthusiastically, he shared his work through his writing. In all, he wrote more than eighty books.

Johannes Kepler broke away from the accepted ideas of his time. In Kepler's day, people could not accurately predict the motions of the planets in the sky. Most Europeans believed that Earth stood still in the center of

A bust portrait of Johannes Kepler. (Note the misspelling of his last name as "Keppler.")

the universe. Kepler's discoveries eventually changed this view.

Kepler showed that planets travel in paths around the sun. He showed that each planet follows its same path over and over. From his discoveries, people could begin to understand the vast distances in our solar system. His discoveries explained how the planets are arranged in space. They showed that natural laws determine the speed at which the planets move. As a result of Kepler's discoveries, the movements of the planets could be predicted with 100 times greater accuracy than before.[3]

In his quest to find the plan of the universe, Kepler discovered three laws of planetary motion. These laws explain basic truths about the paths of Earth, other planets, moons, comets, and satellites in space. These laws apply both in our solar system and in planetary systems around other stars.

Kepler's first law explains the shape of planetary paths. It shows the sun's critical place in the planets' orbits. This law reveals how Pluto can sometimes be closer than Neptune to the sun. It shows why Earth is 91,405,436 miles from the sun in January, but is 94,511,989 miles from it in July.

Kepler's second law shows how far a planet moves over a certain period of time. When they are near the sun, planets move faster. When they are farther away, they move slower. The second law explains why winter on Earth's Northern Hemisphere is several days shorter than summer.

Kepler discovered his third law of planetary motion thirteen years after the first two. Kepler's third law explains the relationship between the length of time it takes a planet to complete one orbit and its distance from the sun. It explains why distant Pluto—a planet Kepler did not even know existed—moves an average of 2.9 miles per second in its orbit. Mercury, the planet closest to the sun, travels an average of 29.7 miles in one second. This law explains why a communications satellite that stays over the same point on Earth must orbit about one hundred times higher than the International Space Station. Kepler's third law makes it possible for scientists to set the speed of the International Space Station, send men to the moon, and launch space probes to Mars and beyond. The third law also helps scientists discover planetary systems around other stars.

Astronomy was Kepler's chief interest, but his curiosity led him to other pursuits as well. He wrote about snowflakes and why they always have six sides. When Galileo used a telescope and observed the moons of Jupiter, Kepler wanted to know how this marvelous device worked. This led Kepler to discoveries about optics, the science of light. Thinking so much about space, he even wrote an imaginary story about a trip to the moon. This book is believed to be the first work of science fiction ever written.

Kepler's love of knowledge and his dedication to the pursuit of answers led to many advances in science. His work gave us a better understanding of Earth's place in the universe. In the fields of astronomy and mathematics, he is considered a great pioneer. For these reasons, Johannes Kepler is widely viewed as one of the most important scientific minds of all time.

Childhood

ROUND STONE TOWERS STOOD AT THE
gates of Weil der Stadt. Inside the city wall,
houses with steep roofs lined narrow cobblestone
streets. About 200 burghers and their families
lived there. Burghers were citizens, or free men.
Townspeople shopped in Weil's market square.
They filled buckets with water from the fountain
there and hauled it home to cook and clean. On
top of the fountain stood a statue of Charles V,
Emperor of the Holy Roman Empire.

Nearby, the three steeples of the Roman
Catholic Church of Saints Peter and Paul

towered over the town rooftops. Most people in Weil were Catholic and worshipped there.

On a narrow street between the market square and the church sat the house of Sebald Kepler, the city's mayor. The Kepler house was a busy place. Red-faced Sebald, his wife, and several of their children lived there. In 1571, the household included their son, Heinrich, and his bride.[1] Heinrich and Katharina were expecting a baby.

Weil der Stadt is located in what is now southern Germany. In the 1500s this region was a part of the Holy Roman Empire.

The Holy Roman Empire was made up of several kingdoms and territories. The ruling nobles of these regions met in councils and elected the emperor. The emperor was a king or prince and was a member of this small group of nobles. The territories of the Holy Roman Empire included lands that are now in Germany, Austria, Switzerland, the Czech Republic, Italy, and France.

Within the Empire were cities that did not belong to surrounding territories. Weil was one

A map showing the boundaries of central Europe as they existed in the time of Johannes Kepler.

of those cities. Just outside the city walls were the lands of the dukes of Württemberg.

Europe in the 1500s was alive with change. This period is now known as the Renaissance. *Renaissance* comes from the Latin word for "rebirth." During this time, ancient Greek and Roman art, literature, and ideas were rediscovered. Some of this teaching was about astronomy and mathematics. Art and learning flourished in the Renaissance. New discoveries and inventions emerged. Many universities and schools opened.

New religious beliefs were also changing Europe. Religion and government were very tightly interwoven. In 1500, the Roman Catholic Church was the main religion of Europe. However, many people were dissatisfied. They felt the Church had moved away from its original teachings. Some princes and dukes thought that the Church had too much control over their lands.

In 1517, a Catholic monk named Martin Luther objected to some of the Roman Catholic Church's practices. He particularly objected to the church's sale of indulgences. With indulgences, people paid money to the church believing that their payment pardoned them from sin.

Luther believed that complete faith in Jesus Christ was the most important part of religion. The Catholic Church did not accept Luther's complaints or his views. The pope, the leader of the Roman Catholic Church, excommunicated him. That meant Luther was no longer a member of the church. Still, Luther continued to write about his religious beliefs. Many people liked his teachings and followed him in starting a new church. People who followed Luther's teachings became known as Lutherans.

When the Lutherans protested their poor treatment by the Catholic rulers, they were called Protestants. Other religious groups split from the Roman Catholic Church, too. Followers of these religions were also called Protestants. Within forty years of Martin Luther's objections, nearly half of Europe was Protestant.[2]

In the territories of the Holy Roman Empire, some princes and dukes joined the new

Lutheran Church. Lutheran churches were officially recognized in the Holy Roman Empire in 1555 in an agreement known as the Peace of Augsburg.[3] Under this agreement, princes and dukes could decide the religion of their territory. The people in their lands were expected to follow their rulers' church.

The dukes of Württemberg were Lutheran. The Lutheran Church became the religion of their lands. The city of Weil der Stadt, however, was Roman Catholic. Although the Keplers lived in Weil, they were Lutheran.

On December 27, 1571, in Weil, Heinrich and Katharina Kepler's first child entered the world. Johannes Kepler was not born into a happy home.

"Criminally inclined, quarrelsome and liable to a bad end," were some of Heinrich Kepler's traits, his son Johannes later wrote. Heinrich treated his wife badly. Katharina was argumentative and stubborn.[4] "Treated shabbily," Johannes wrote, "she could not overcome the inhumanity of her husband."[5] Anger and unhappiness ruled their marriage.

The house where Johannes Kepler was born, which stood on this site in Weil der Stadt, burned down in 1648. However, this house—built shortly after in the same location—is believed to have the same appearance and form as Kepler's original home.

Living with Heinrich's parents probably made their marriage even worse. Sebald Kepler was respected as mayor, but he could be arrogant and obstinate. His wife was "clever, deceitful, blazing with hatred, the queen of busy-bodies," according to notes Johannes Kepler later wrote.[6]

Our knowledge of the Kepler personalities comes from notes Johannes Kepler wrote when he was about twenty-five years old. Despite his family's shortcomings, Kepler was devoted to them. As an adult, he studied his parents' and grandparents' birth horoscopes. He was trying to see if astrology explained their bad qualities.[7] A birth horoscope is an astrological interpretation of the heavens at the time a baby is born. Astrologers believe that the positions of the planets, sun, and moon at birth shape a person's character for life.

Before Johannes Kepler was three years old, his father left Weil. Heinrich joined an army in the Netherlands as a mercenary soldier. A mercenary soldier is one who is paid to fight for a country other than his own. Heinrich liked the excitement of battle and war.[8] To his family's embarrassment, in the Netherlands he was fighting against Protestants, people of the Keplers' religion.[9]

For Katharina Kepler, life with Sebald and his wife was miserable. A year after Heinrich left, Katharina followed him. Johannes was left with his grandparents. They treated him roughly.[10] During this time, Johannes caught smallpox. Smallpox was a deadly disease that affected most people in Europe in the 1500s. Smallpox started with aches, fever, and a rash. The rash turned to pox—spots that looked like pimples. After a few days the pox scabbed over. When the scabs fell off, they left scars. The disease also often caused blindness. Kepler's eyesight was damaged when he had smallpox. He never saw well afterward.

Katharina and Heinrich Kepler eventually returned, but they did not stay in Weil. They moved with their children to Leonberg, a city in Württemberg.

The move to Leonberg was good for Johannes. The dukes of Württemberg had opened Latin schools for Protestant students in many towns. These schools were superior to the local German schools. Latin was the language of higher education and culture at the time. The goal of the Latin schools was to raise educated Protestant citizens. Students who continued their education could hold government positions or become pastors in the church when they became adults. When he was seven years old, Johannes Kepler entered Leonberg's Latin school.

The Kepler family's life remained unsettled. Heinrich never found a career. He joined foreign armies and fought in battles. He briefly owned an inn. Once, he had legal problems and was nearly hanged. When Johannes was seventeen, Heinrich left to fight again. He never returned.[11]

Johannes Kepler took after his mother in some ways. Both were small and slight with dark hair. Katharina Kepler was intense and restless. Apparently she had a very active mind and many interests. She collected plants and made herbal medicines.[12] (Katharina Kepler's interest in herbs and potions would later be used against her when she was accused of witchcraft.)

In many ways, Johannes Kepler's childhood was unhappy. He was often sick. His family life was unstable. However, experiences with each of his parents made lasting impressions.

One night in the winter of 1577, Katharina Kepler took her young son outside. They climbed a long hill together, then stopped and looked up.[13] A fuzzy ball of light glowed in the night sky. Behind it flowed a shimmering tail. The tail stretched one fifth of the way across the heavens.

Around the world people gazed at the Great Comet of 1577. Some thought it was an omen. They thought it predicted disease or war. On a small island in Denmark, the astronomer Tycho Brahe saw and studied this comet. Night after night, he measured its movement against the background stars.

The little boy in Germany and the Danish nobleman would eventually meet. Their shared love of astronomy would have spectacular results.

The second celestial event Kepler remembered from his childhood he saw with his father.

Heinrich took him outdoors one night in 1580 to see a lunar eclipse.[14] A lunar eclipse occurs when Earth passes directly between the sun and moon. Together, father and son watched Earth's shadow glide across the face of the full moon.

Johannes Kepler excelled in school. He learned to read, write, and speak Latin. He memorized Latin grammar rules and recited Latin poems and plays. His family life was still very chaotic. At times he missed months of school. With these many interruptions, it took him five years to complete the three-year school program.

When he finally finished Latin school, Kepler took an examination to see if he could continue his studies. He passed the test and was accepted in the Lutheran seminary in Adelberg as a scholarship student. His parents did not need to pay for his education. A seminary is a school where students are trained in religion. By age thirteen, Johannes Kepler was on track to become a Lutheran pastor.

Discovering Copernicus

"KEPLER HAS SUCH A SUPERIOR AND magnificent mind that something special may be expected of him," the school administrators at the University of Tübingen wrote.[1] They approved his request to continue his scholarship.

Johannes Kepler was seventeen years old when he began his studies in Tübingen. He was enrolled in a five-year program to become a Lutheran pastor. For the first two years he took classes in a variety of subjects. His studies included astronomy, mathematics, physics, ancient Greek, and Hebrew. Three years of religious training followed.

At Tübingen, Kepler was serious and competitive. The university still has the records of his grades—straight A's.[2]

Throughout Kepler's school years, he looked forward to his future in the church. He prayed often. He memorized long psalms and studied church doctrines.[3] He thought about the meaning of the church's teachings. In his private thoughts, he questioned a few of these beliefs. The intolerance of different faiths for each other troubled him.[4]

Kepler enjoyed student life. He had friends. He was apparently involved in some pranks. He performed in school plays. Women did not study at the school. Even if they did, women did not act in theater at that time. Female characters were performed by men. Kepler was small and slight, so he was cast in women's roles in the school productions. Kepler wrote about one particular religious play. He played a character named Marianne. The students performed outdoors in the market square in February 1591.[5]

One of Kepler's professors, Michael Mästlin, taught a theory that sent Kepler's mind soaring.

Mästlin taught mathematics, which included astronomy.

"I was disturbed by the many difficulties of the usual conception of the universe, and I was so delighted by Copernicus, whom Mr. Mästlin often mentioned in his lectures," Kepler later recalled.[6] Kepler was thrilled with the theory of Polish scholar and church official Nicolaus Copernicus.

In Kepler's time, the sun, moon, five known planets, and stars were believed to revolve around Earth in crystal spheres. The stars were believed to be on the largest sphere, far from Earth. Each of the five known planets supposedly had its own sphere. The spheres were arranged one inside the other. There were only five planets in this plan, because only Mercury, Venus, Mars, Jupiter, and Saturn can be seen without the aid of a powerful telescope. Uranus, Neptune, and Pluto were not discovered until long after Kepler's death. The sun and moon also were believed to revolve around Earth on crystal spheres. Earth was not considered a

The seminary at the University of Tübingen, where Kepler studied from 1589 until 1594.

planet. Earth supposedly stood still at the center of this enormous mechanism.

This model of the universe had been accepted for centuries. It was not questioned by many Europeans. Aristotle, an ancient Greek philosopher, had written about this view of the universe in the fourth century B.C. Certain ideas were basic in this plan. First was that Earth was at the center of the universe. The second idea was that all movement in the heavens is uniform circular motion. This means that all heavenly objects, the sun, moon, and stars were believed to move at constant speeds in perfectly circular patterns.

In some ways, this plan made sense. People could not feel the Earth move, so it was easy to believe that it stood still. On Earth, it looks like the sun and moon move. The stars are such great distances from Earth that they appear to move together as though they are on an enormous steadily turning sphere. Today, even though we know that millions and millions of miles separate the stars, their observed positions are still described as though they were on a sphere.

There were problems making this plan agree with what people observed in the sky. The movement of the five planets was too confusing to be easily explained. Anyone who watched the sky knew that Mercury and Venus are only seen in the evening and early morning. These two planets are always close to the sun. They are never seen late at night. Mars, Jupiter, and Saturn can be seen any time of night. They usually move slowly, night to night, west to east against the background stars. Sometimes, though, a planet appears to reverse its direction and move the other way. This is called retrograde motion. Also, the planets sometimes appear to move faster than at other times.

The Greeks believed the planets were stars, but called them wandering stars. The word *planet* comes from the Greek word for "wanderer."

Ptolemy, another Greek philosopher, wrote a detailed book about Aristotle's model. The book is known as the *Almagest*. In Arabic, *Almagest* means "the greatest." Ptolemy wrote the *Almagest* in about 150 A.D. It was the most important book about astronomy for many centuries. Ptolemy's book had explanations for many of the planets' movements, including retrograde motion. It also had an explanation for why the planets seem to move faster and slower.

Ptolemy explained that smaller circles, like little wheels, turned on the larger spheres. The small circles were called epicycles. The planets supposedly traveled on these epicycles. Altogether, Ptolemy's universe had fifty-five turning epicycles and spheres. With some complicated calculations, Ptolemy's model could explain retrograde motion.

Besides dealing with retrograde motion, Ptolemy provided an answer to another question that troubled observers. This question was why the planets sometimes appear to move faster at different times. Ptolemy suggested that Earth was not exactly at the center of the spheres. He suggested that Earth was a small distance from the center. Exactly on the other side of the center, he claimed there was an invisible balancing point, called an equant. Moving the Earth from the exact center of the system helped explain the apparent change of speed of the planets.

For centuries, Ptolemy's calculations were used to predict the positions of the planets. Over the years, though, it became clear that they were not completely reliable. Still, the Roman Catholic Church accepted Ptolemy's model.

Some church officials believed the Bible said that Earth stood still and the sun moved. Ptolemy's plan became the church's accepted view of the universe.

In the early 1500s, Nicolaus Copernicus had a different idea. He saw another way to explain retrograde motion. This idea had once been suggested by an ancient Greek philosopher named Aristarchus. Aristarchus's writings had disappeared over the centuries. Only a few mentions of his theory survived.

Copernicus, like Aristarchus, suggested that the sun might be at the center of the universe. In Copernicus's model, Earth was a planet. As a planet, Earth traveled around the sun. Earth, he suggested, also rotated. Rotation would explain the daily rising and setting of the sun, moon, stars, and planets. A moving Earth explained retrograde motion. If Earth moved around the sun, then the changing view of the other moving planets would make them sometimes appear to move backward.

Copernicus wrote about his theory. In English, his book's title is *On the Revolutions of the*

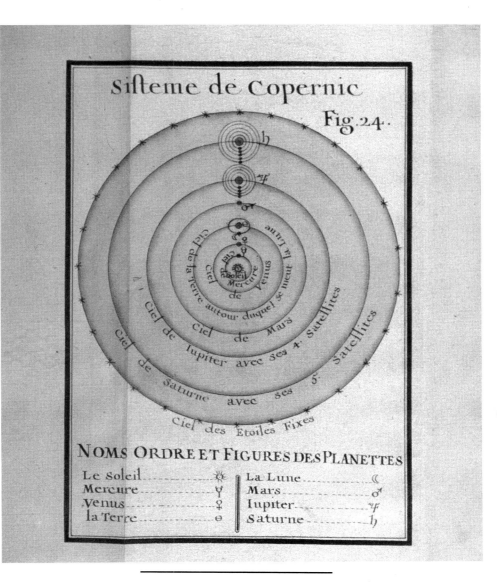

The Copernican plan of the universe. Earth is the third planet from the sun and Copernicus correctly shows the moon revolving around Earth. In this plan, the "Etoiles Fixes" are the stars. They are on the sphere beyond Saturn (Uranus, Neptune and Pluto were not known in Copernicus's time).

Heavenly Spheres. It was published in 1543, the year Copernicus died. His theory was not widely accepted at the time.

Michael Mästlin taught his students at Tübingen about Copernicus's work. One of them, Johannes Kepler, was enthralled. To Kepler, Copernicus's theory made far more sense than the accepted ideas about crystal spheres and epicycles.

Kepler spent time with Mästlin learning about Copernicus's ideas. Then he thought about them and studied them on his own. "I collected, little by little, partly from the words of Mästlin, partly from my own efforts, the advantages which Copernicus has over Ptolemy," Kepler wrote.[7] Kepler debated the benefits of Copernicus's system with other students. He wrote a paper about Earth's rotation.

Kepler was fascinated by these ideas about the universe. Still, he was completely devoted to a future in the clergy. He loved theology (the study of religious faith, God, and God's relationship with the world). He truly wanted to be a pastor in the church.

In 1594, when Kepler was just weeks away from graduating, his life changed. The math teacher at the Protestant School in Graz had died. Graz was a city in Austria about 300 miles from Tübingen. The school asked the University of Tübingen to send a new math teacher. Kepler was clearly gifted at mathematics. School administrators recommended him for the job.

Kepler wanted to be a pastor, not a teacher. He was almost done with his studies. It was an honor that the university recommended him, but not one that he wanted. He asked for advice from his grandfather and his mother. Finally, Kepler accepted the job.

A few weeks later, in April 1594, Kepler was on his way to Graz to teach math and astronomy.

Solids and Spheres

THE PROTESTANT SCHOOL IN GRAZ WAS
a handsome complex of buildings arranged
around a courtyard. Students and some teachers,
including Kepler, lived at the school. Lutheran
noblemen in the region had started the school
for the education of their sons.

Graz was in a region where the ruling family,
including young Prince Ferdinand, was Catholic.
Many Lutherans, however, lived in and around
Graz. For several years, the ruling Catholics had
allowed Lutheran churches in the area. When
Kepler moved to Graz, Catholic tolerance
of Protestants was about to change. Prince

Ferdinand would try to restore the region to the Roman Catholic Church. In the midst of all this, Johannes Kepler began his teaching career.

"The study of mathematics is not everyone's meat," administrators at the Protestant School wrote in a report. They were explaining why very few students took Kepler's classes.[1]

Mathematics was probably not the only reason students stayed away from Kepler's courses. Kepler was enormously enthusiastic about mathematics and astronomy. When he was excited, he talked fast. His active mind jumped from one idea to the next. His lessons changed direction as he leapt between thoughts. Expressions that his students did not understand peppered his lectures.[2]

To add to his teaching salary, Kepler wrote astrological calendars. These calendars predicted events in the coming year. Kepler had mixed feelings about astrology. On the one hand, he believed that the heavens influenced people's lives. On the other, he did not like fortune-telling. He called astrology "the foolish little daughter of the respectable reasonable mother astronomy."[3] Eight hundred birth horoscopes and several astrological calendars written by Kepler still exist.[4]

Kepler's first astrological calendar was for the year 1595. There was a lot of common sense in it. He predicted bitter cold weather and invasions from Turkey. The winter of 1595 was indeed frigid. Rumors claimed that the weather was so cold that people's noses broke off when they blew them.[5] Turkish armies also invaded southern Austria in 1595. Because of their accurate predictions, Kepler's calendars were very popular.

This same year, Kepler's active mind returned to Copernicus. More and more he thought about how the sun-centered universe made sense.

"Finally in the year 1595," Kepler wrote, "when I had a strong desire to rest from my lectures, and to have done with [my teaching] duties . . . I threw myself with the whole force of my mind into the subject."[6] Kepler wanted to figure out the plan of the universe.

"There were three things in particular about

The city of Graz. The school where Kepler taught stood next door to the long, low, gray building at the center of the picture.

which I persistently sought the reason why they were such and not otherwise," wrote Kepler. These were "the number, the size and the motion of the circles."[7] Kepler was following Copernicus's plan as he asked these questions. He believed that the planets, including Earth, revolved around the sun. Each planet's path, he believed, followed a circle within a space on an imaginary sphere. Kepler did not believe there were solid spheres in space.

Kepler's question about the number of planets seems strange to us today. He wanted to know *why* there were six planets. Kepler asked this question because he believed that mathematics was a key to the plan of the universe. He assumed that there was a reason why there were exactly six, "instead of twenty or a hundred."[8]

Like Copernicus, Kepler believed Earth was a planet. When he wrote of six planets, he counted Mercury, Venus, Earth, Mars, Jupiter, and Saturn. Today we know that nine planets revolve around our sun. Uranus, Neptune, and Pluto were discovered long after Kepler's time.

Kepler's second question was about the size of the planets' circles. Kepler correctly thought there were great distances between the planets' paths. With his second question, Kepler was trying to learn the distances that exist in our solar system.

Kepler's third goal was to understand the planets' movements. At times they appeared to move faster and at other times slower. Kepler saw that planets far from the sun, like Jupiter and Saturn, traveled slower than those close to the sun, like Mercury and Venus. Kepler believed that a force from the sun accounted for planetary motion. Kepler is considered the first scientist to look for a cause of the planets' movements.

For several months, Kepler looked for answers to his questions. He used mathematics in his search. In one attempt, he looked for a simple explanation for the planets' distances. Mercury is the closest planet to the sun. He wondered if Venus, the second planet from the sun, was twice as far from the sun as Mercury, and if Earth, the third planet, was three times as far.[9] When he checked this idea with observations of the planets, he saw that it was wrong. Then he tried other ideas.

In July 1595, Kepler changed his search. He decided that geometry might answer some of his questions. Geometry is the branch of mathematics that looks at points, lines, and shapes and how they relate to each other in space.

In this investigation he discovered something

extraordinary. He believed that he had found the secret of the universe. Kepler believed that the spacing between the planets was explained by different geometric shapes.

A way to understand Kepler's theory is to imagine you have round bowls and cardboard boxes of several different sizes. Imagine putting a box inside the largest bowl. The corners of the box must touch the inside of the bowl. Inside the box, place another bowl. This bowl must fit so that it touches each flat side of the box. In your imaginary model, continue alternating smaller bowls and boxes. Altogether, you would use six bowls, one for each planet Kepler knew. Five boxes would take up space between the bowls.

Kepler's model was similar to this. The planets' orbits were defined by the bowls. The boxes determined the space between the spheres. Saturn's path, for example, would be defined by the largest bowl, Jupiter's by the second bowl, and so on.

In Kepler's model, the shapes and spheres alternated. Certain special shapes explained the spacing of the spheres. Kepler knew that in geometry there are five shapes called "perfect solids." All the faces of a perfect solid are identical. A cube, for example, has six square faces. A tetrahedron, which looks like a pyramid, has four identical triangular faces.

When Kepler mathematically used these perfect solids to explain the spaces between the spheres, he found an arrangement that worked with considerable accuracy.[10] He was elated. The relative distances between the planets seemed to work. Also, there were exactly five of these special shapes. To Kepler, this agreed perfectly with his idea that there was a mathematical plan of the universe. Five perfect solids fit exactly between six spheres.

Kepler's model of solids and spheres works surprisingly well to explain the relative distances of the planets' paths from the sun and from each other. In other words, if you expanded his model to the size of the solar system, some of the planets would travel fairly close to the spheres. Today we don't see Kepler's geometric model as the explanation for the arrangement of the solar

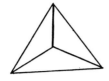 **Tetrahedron: Four faces, all triangles**

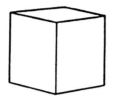 **Cube: Six faces, all squares**

 **Octahedron: Eight faces, all triangles**

 **Dodecahedron: Twelve faces, all pentagons**

 **Icosahedron: Twenty faces, all triangles**

The five "perfect solids" in geometry.

system. It was just a coincidence that the "perfect solids" fit so well.

Kepler, though, was convinced. "What delight I have found in this discovery I shall never be able to express in words," he wrote. "No longer did I regret the wasted time; I was no longer sick of the toil. . . ."[11] With renewed energy and determination he set out to prove his discovery. He used observations of the planets to test his theory. Kepler's belief in his discovery would guide the rest of his life. It would lead him to true discoveries about the shape, spacing, and movements of our solar system.

Kepler immediately wrote to his teacher, Michael Mästlin, at the University of Tübingen about his discovery. Then Kepler wrote a book to share his idea with the world. Mästlin would help him get it published.

Kepler called his book *Mysterium Cosmographicum*. This translates into English as "The Secret of the Universe." He wrote the book in Latin. In it, Kepler explained his theory in detail. *Mysterium Cosmographicum* was the first book to attempt to prove the theory of the sun-centered universe since Copernicus's own work. Inserted in each copy of Kepler's book was a large folded sheet of smooth paper. Unfolded, the page displayed an illustration of Kepler's solids and spheres.

To cover printing costs, the publisher required Kepler to buy 200 copies of the book.[12] Kepler sent them to scholars around Europe. He sent one to Galileo Galilei in Italy. He sent the book to mathematicians at German universities. He wanted to be sure that Tycho Brahe, the famous astronomer, read it, so he sent two copies to him.

More than 400 years later, a very few copies of those original 1597 books still exist. Each one is now very valuable. They are valuable not just because they are old. They are treasured because the ideas in the book grew to change humanity's knowledge of the universe.

While the book was being published, Kepler went to Tübingen. He met with Michael Mästlin and his publisher. He also went to make a proposal to the dukes of Württemberg.[13]

Kepler suggested that the dukes might want

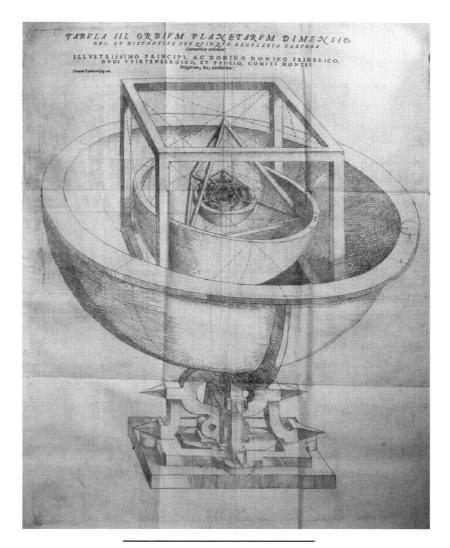

An illustration of Kepler's model of the planetary spheres as presented in his first book, Mysterium Cosmographicum. *Kepler believed that the mathematical proportions of certain geometric shapes explained the relative distances between the planetary spheres. Spheres and different "perfect solids" alternate down to Mercury, the closest planet to the sun, which is at the center.*

to pay for a silver model of his solids and spheres. The planets could be represented by diamonds, pearls, and gems. The model, he suggested, could be designed so that each sphere would hold a different beverage. One would hold wine, others could contain brandy, mead, and water. The dukes were interested, but apparently the model was never made.

Kepler was away from Graz for several months, but he was eager to return. He had met Barbara Müller, the "plump and pretty" daughter of a wealthy family there.[14] Barbara was twenty-three years old. She had already been widowed twice. She had a young daughter. Barbara's parents were not thrilled with Kepler as a suitor. He was quite poor. As a teacher, he had little social prestige. Eventually, though, they gave their permission.

When Kepler returned to Graz, they married. They moved from the school into a house of their own in Graz. As they started their lives together, Kepler's *Mysterium Cosmographicum* was reaching scholars around Europe.

Turmoil and Tycho

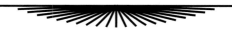

"IN ASTRONOMY," TYCHO BRAHE WROTE, "it is first of all necessary to obtain very many observations taken over a long period of time by means of instruments that are not liable to error."[1] For thirty-eight years, Tycho studied the heavens. He designed the best astronomical instruments of the time. With these instruments, he took thousands of observations of the sun, moon, planets, stars, and comets.

Telescopes were not among Tycho Brahe's astronomical instruments. The telescope was invented nine years after he died. With his instruments, Tycho measured exactly where objects in space were observed. Many of his measurements were accurate to about one fifteenth the apparent diameter of the full moon.

Tycho's goal was to "lay the foundations of and develop a renewed astronomy."[2] He believed the way to achieve his goal was to collect observations first and then interpret them. Kepler's approach was exactly the opposite. Kepler started with ideas. After he carefully thought out an idea, he used observations to see if they proved it.

King Frederick II of Denmark supported Tycho and his astronomy. Frederick gave him an island and money to build a castle observatory. An observatory is a building designed for astronomical research. Tycho built Uraniborg. *Uraniborg* means "Castle of the Heavens." Observing instruments stood in its towers and in special observation rooms. Assistants came to Tycho's island to study the heavens with him.

While Kepler was publishing *Mysterium Cosmographicum*, Tycho's life was changing. King Frederick II died. The new king would not support Tycho or Uraniborg. Tycho decided to leave Denmark. He took his observations with him. He was staying at a friend's castle in Germany when he received Kepler's book.

When Tycho read *Mysterium Cosmographicum*, he was impressed. He thought Kepler's solids and spheres were a clever idea.[3] Tycho could see that Kepler was a capable mathematician.[4] Tycho wrote an encouraging letter to Kepler and suggested they meet. "Here you may discuss such lofty topics with me face to face in an agreeable and pleasant manner."[5]

Tycho did not agree with all of Kepler's ideas. He did not believe that Earth moved. He could not accept Copernicus's theory that Earth revolved around the sun. Tycho had his own theory. In Tycho's system, Mercury, Venus, Mars, Jupiter, and Saturn revolved around the sun. The sun, with the planets, then traveled around Earth. It was a complicated explanation.

From Germany, Tycho was going to Prague, home of the emperor of the Holy Roman Empire. Prague was only a few days' journey from Graz.

A portrait of Danish astronomer Tycho Brahe.

In Graz, meanwhile, the political and religious situation was changing. The region's Catholic prince, Ferdinand, had traveled to Rome and visited the pope. In Rome, Ferdinand supposedly vowed to restore Catholicism to his region.[6]

"Everything trembles," Kepler wrote, "in anticipation of the return of the prince. . . . Everywhere one hears threats."[7] Kepler, as a Lutheran, worried about what the prince would do. Would Ferdinand still allow Protestants to live in Graz?

When Ferdinand returned, many Protestants

were angry with him and his beliefs. Some circulated unkind cartoons of the pope. Two of the town's Lutheran preachers ridiculed Catholic beliefs during their church services. Their words and actions enraged Ferdinand.[8]

On September 19, 1598, Prince Ferdinand ordered all Protestant preachers and teachers to leave Graz. The prince closed the school where Kepler taught. Soldiers came into town to enforce the order. On September 28, the Protestants had to leave town by sunset "at the cost of life and limb."[9]

Kepler, the pastors, and the other teachers departed. Barbara Kepler stayed in Graz. She did not want to leave her home. Her family was there and so was her inheritance of buildings and land.

Although Kepler was a Protestant, Ferdinand allowed him to return after a few weeks. Without teaching duties, Kepler had time to think about the plan of the universe. He wanted to write several books about the mathematical beauty of the universe. One book would be about the movement of the planets. Another would be about the sun and the stars. Kepler planned to call this work the *Harmonice Mundi* (the "Harmony of the World.")[10]

During this time, Kepler did more calculations of the planets' positions in his model of the solids and spheres. He was troubled about some of his results. When he used observations to calculate Jupiter's sphere, the answers did not match his theory as closely as he wanted. It was not a huge difference, but Kepler demanded great accuracy. He decided that better observations would help him find the explanation for this difference. Kepler knew that Tycho Brahe had the observations he needed.

In the meantime, sadness came into Johannes and Barbara Kepler's lives. In February 1598, their first child was born. To the parents' great sorrow, the baby died two months later. The following year the Keplers' second child was born. She died when she was only thirty-five days old.

The religious situation in Graz had been growing steadily worse. Lutheran churches were no longer permitted there. Singing Protestant hymns was forbidden. Graz children were supposed to be baptized in the Catholic church. Because the Keplers did not baptize their baby girl in the Catholic church, they had to pay a fine in order to bury her.[11]

Kepler decided that it was time to leave Graz. He wrote to the University of Tübingen to see if they had a job for him. They did not. Instead, he set out to meet Tycho Brahe. Barbara Kepler again stayed behind. She would wait in Graz while he found work and a new place to live.

Tycho Brahe had arrived in Prague. He was getting settled into the castle of Benatky there. Rudolph II, emperor of the Holy Roman Empire, had appointed Tycho to be his Imperial Mathematician. Rudolph promised Tycho an enormous salary, although he never actually paid it all. As Imperial Mathematician, Tycho could continue to study the heavens. The Imperial Mathematician was also expected to cast horoscopes and write astrological calendars for the emperor.

Tycho was delighted that Kepler was coming to see him. He invited Kepler immediately to his castle. "You will come not so much as a guest but as a very welcome friend and highly desirable participant and companion in our observations of the heavens," he wrote.[12]

On February 4, 1600, Tycho Brahe and Johannes Kepler met. Each man had a vision of the universe. Each one also wanted something from the other. Kepler wanted Tycho's observations. He wanted to use them to refine his plan of the sun-centered universe. Tycho wanted Kepler's assistance with astronomical computations. He believed that the calculations from his observations would prove his theory of an Earth-centered system.[13]

Kepler moved into Benatky Castle to work with Tycho. They were a strange pair: two exiles who shared a passion for astronomy. They had little else in common.

Tycho was fifty-three years old, a wealthy and self-confident nobleman. He wore the clothes of his aristocratic rank: formal black cloaks, gold necklaces, and white ruffed collars. His appearance was grand and somewhat fearsome. Tycho's nose was made of metal. His natural nose was cut off in a duel during his college days. Tycho was famous and somewhat arrogant. He was accustomed to having many assistants who followed his orders.

Kepler was young, thoughtful, and small. He was a commoner with little money. Kepler was, however, very intelligent and extremely determined. He sometimes described himself as a snappy little dog.[14] Kepler was thoroughly committed to the Copernican theory that all the planets, including Earth, revolved around the sun. He was driven by his need to find answers. Kepler expected to be treated as Tycho's equal.

The relationship between the two men was sometimes stormy. As they negotiated where Kepler would live and what he would be paid, it sometimes seemed as if they would never agree. The storms fortunately passed.

Tycho had thousands of observations. Long and tedious calculations were required to plot them as points on a plan of the universe. Tycho's assistants usually did much of this work. During Kepler's first few weeks at Benatky, Tycho assigned him to work on the path of Mars.

Kepler was a gifted mathematician. He expected to figure out the path of Mars in eight days.

However, after several months of working on the Mars calculations with Tycho, Kepler went back to Graz. He hoped to do his research there and keep in touch with Tycho by letter. In Graz, he found that the religious situation was horrible. All citizens of the city were required to become Catholic. Anyone who did not was banished. Kepler did not agree with all the teaching of the Lutheran Church, but changing his religion was not an option for him. He wrote again to Tycho.

"Do not linger, hurry here with confidence as rapidly as possible," Tycho wrote back.[15] Johannes Kepler, his wife, and his stepdaughter left Graz with two wagons full of their household belongings. They were going to Prague.

In Prague, Tycho was ready to proceed with an ambitious project. He wanted to compile tables of planetary movement. These would require plotting the paths of all the planets. The project, he assumed, would prove his Tychonic system. He believed the calculations would show that the sun and planets revolved around Earth. Kepler was still working on Mars.

In September 1601, Tycho took Kepler to meet Emperor Rudolph. Tycho told the emperor about the tables. He explained that Kepler would assist him. Tycho asked permission to name the project in the emperor's honor—the *Rudolphine Tables*. Rudolph was pleased.

Less than a month later, Tycho fell ill. In great pain he tossed with fever and sleeplessness. Kepler was with him much of the time. As Tycho lay dying, he begged Kepler to prove the Tychonic system.[16]

Tycho Brahe died October 24, 1601. Two days later, Emperor Rudolph appointed Johannes Kepler to the position of Imperial Mathematician of the Holy Roman Empire. Kepler would write the *Rudolphine Tables*. He would work on them for almost all the rest of his life.

Two Laws of
Planetary Motion

BEFORE KEPLER TACKLED THE HUGE project of writing the *Rudolphine Tables* he needed to finish his work on the path of Mars. The tables would include information about all the planets. Kepler correctly believed that whatever he learned about Mars would be true for the other planets as well.

Kepler called it his "war with Mars."[1] He found humor in his pun. Mars, the fourth planet from the sun, is named for the Roman god of war.

At first, Kepler expected the Mars calculations to take a few days. When Tycho died more than a year later, Kepler was still working on Mars. He would puzzle over the path of Mars for more than five years.

To solve the problem of the path of Mars, Kepler had excellent tools. He had Tycho's marvelous observations. Tycho had measured the positions of Mars for twenty years. Kepler had his own outstanding mathematical ability. Finally, he had great determination. He was convinced that he would find answers. He would keep trying until he succeeded.

When Kepler began searching for the path of Mars, he expected a circle would define the planet's orbit around the sun. Circles and spheres had been part of the understanding of the universe for centuries. In this way, Kepler's thoughts were similar to the accepted ideas of his time.

Kepler also had some ideas about Mars that were different from the accepted views of his time. Like Copernicus, he thought that the sun was at or near the center of the solar system. (Most people still believed in an Earth-centered universe.) Kepler believed that a force from the sun caused the movement of the planets. He thought that the sun's force was stronger on planets when they were close to it and weaker when they were farther away.[2]

Kepler started his search with much information about Mars. He knew that the orbital period of Mars was slightly less than 687 days.[3] A planet's orbital period is another name for a planet's year. The orbital period is the time it takes the planet to travel around the sun and return to the same point in space. Earth's orbital period is about 365 days. Kepler knew that Mars, like the other planets, appears to move faster at some times than at others. This apparent change of speed had been known by the ancient Greeks and Copernicus.

To understand some of the difficulty in deciphering Mars, let us look at one piece of Kepler's study. Kepler believed that Earth was a planet moving around the sun. If Earth was moving, he realized, then Tycho's observations were taken from different places along Earth's path. In other words, the observations of Mars were taken from different places in space. How could he discover Mars's true position with both Earth and Mars moving?

Fortunately, Tycho had many observations of Mars. Kepler knew the 687-day orbital period of Mars. Kepler correctly believed that Mars would be in the same place in space every 687 days, even though Earth would be in a different position along its own orbit. Kepler started using Tycho's observations of Mars in pairs taken 687 days apart.[4] This approach required complex calculations, but it was successful.

Using pairs of Mars observations, Kepler tried to find a circular path for Mars. In geometry, if you know the positions of three points, you can draw a circle that passes through all three. After some calculations, Kepler had three points. From those points, he drew a circle. If the circle correctly described the path of Mars, then the other observations would fall on the same circle. The new points, however, did not. They were close to the circle, but not exactly on it. To understand how close they were, look at the moon. The observations missed Kepler's circle by less than one quarter of the apparent diameter of the full moon.

A sloppy mathematician might have decided that the other points were close enough or that Tycho's observations were not right. Kepler, however, demanded precision. He had faith in the accuracy of Tycho's work. Instead of accepting this error, Kepler kept looking.

Kepler's "war with Mars" lasted from 1600 to 1605. One thousand pages of his handwritten calculations of Mars still exist. He kept working and trying new ways to find Mars's path. He was constantly testing his work with Tycho's observations. Although Kepler had certain ideas when he started, he changed his ideas when the math and observations proved an idea was wrong.

In 1605, Kepler found the path of Mars.

"O ridiculous me!" he wrote, "no figure is left for the planet to follow other than a perfectly elliptical one."[5] Elliptical means in the shape of an ellipse, which is a sort of flattened circle.

In Kepler's search for the path of Mars, he discovered two laws of planetary motion. These

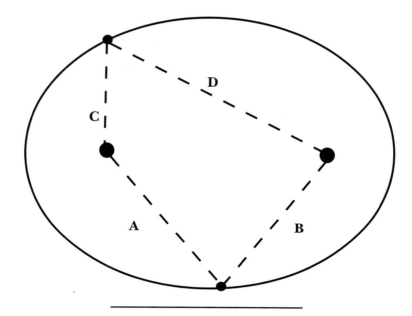

Kepler discovered that the paths of the planets are elliptical (shaped like ellipses). An ellipse has two foci. The sum of the distances from the foci to any point on the ellipse is exactly equal. In other words, A+B is the same length as C+D.

laws describe certain facts about the planets and the way they move.

Kepler wrote a book about his war with Mars. It is known as the *Astronomia Nova*, or "New Astronomy." Kepler's first two laws of planetary motion are in this book.

Kepler's first law of planetary motion says: "The orbit of each planet around the sun is an ellipse with the sun at one focus of the ellipse."[6]

An ellipse looks like a stretched out circle.

Ellipses can be almost round or very flat. Each planet in our solar system follows an elliptical path around the sun.

One way to understand ellipses is to first think about circles. A circle surrounds one center point. Every point on the circle is the same distance from the center. An ellipse surrounds two points. Each of these points is called a focus. (The plural of *focus* is *foci*.) The sum of the distances from any point on the ellipse to the two foci is equal.[7] The roundness or flatness of an ellipse is called its eccentricity. Round ellipses have low eccentricity. Flat ellipses have high eccentricity.

Kepler's first law of planetary motion has two parts. First, it explains that the planets do not travel in circles. This was a big break from the accepted ideas of Ptolemy and even Copernicus. This discovery of Kepler's revealed the true shape of the planets' paths in space. Understanding that planets follow elliptical paths rather than circular ones would make it possible to more accurately explain retrograde motion, the apparent backward movement of the planets.

Kepler's first law also showed that the sun was in a critical place in the orbit of each planet. The planets' orbits are all different sizes. They also all have different elliptical shapes. Some planets' orbits are flatter and some are rounder. However, for every planet in our solar system,

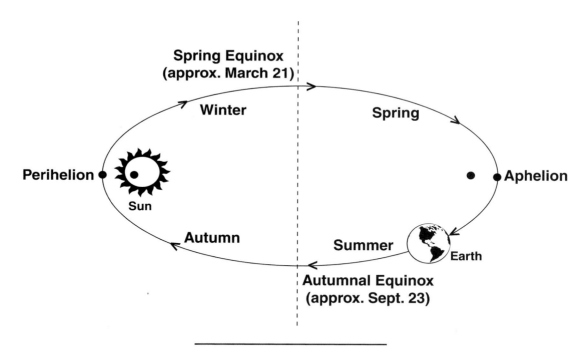

Kepler's first law explains that the orbit of each planet is an ellipse with the sun at one focus. In this diagram, the orbit of the earth is exaggerated to appear flatter than it really is.

the sun is in a special place. It is at one focus of each planet's orbit.

It was good fortune that Tycho assigned Kepler to study Mars. Mars's elliptical orbit is flatter than any of the other planets except Pluto and Mercury. Mars's orbit is much flatter than the orbital paths of Earth, Venus, Jupiter, or Saturn. If Kepler had studied one of those planets instead, he might not have realized that the points did not fall exactly on the circle.

Since each planet follows an elliptical path, but the sun stays still at one focus, each planet's distance from the sun changes as the planet follows its path. Sometimes the planet is close to the sun. At other times it is farther away. A planet's closest point to the sun is its perihelion. Its farthest point is its aphelion. For example, Mars is 128,400,000 miles from the sun at perihelion. At aphelion, Mars is 154,900,000 miles from it.

Pluto has the flattest orbital path of all the planets. Its orbit is so eccentric that Pluto sometimes crosses inside the path of Neptune's orbit. Usually Pluto is the farthest planet from the sun. However, for 20 years of its 249-year orbital period, Pluto is actually closer than Neptune to the sun.

Before Kepler discovered planets' elliptical paths, he tried many, many ways to solve the problem of Mars's path. One of these yielded surprising results.

Kepler believed that the sun must be in an important place in each planet's orbit. He thought that understanding the changing speed of Mars was a key to solving his problem. Kepler plotted how far Mars traveled over specific periods of time. This effort led him to discover his second law of planetary motion.

Kepler's second law of planetary motion says: "A straight line joining the center of a planet and the center of the sun sweeps over equal areas in equal times as the planet travels around its orbit."[8]

This law means that planets move faster when they are near the sun and slower when they are farther away. It also explains how to calculate how much faster or slower the planet moves at different points along its path.

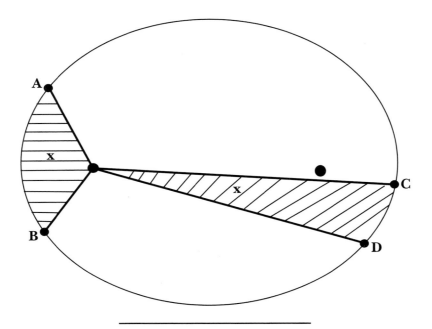

An illustration of Kepler's second law, which states that a straight line between the sun and a planet will sweep across equal areas in equal periods of time. When a planet is closer to the sun, it will travel more quickly over a greater distance (as in AB). When farther from the sun, it travels more slowly and covers a short distance (as in CD). The areas (×) are equal.

As a planet follows its orbit, it is constantly changing speed. When a planet is close to the sun, it moves faster than when it is farther away. A planet will also travel a different distance over the same period of time depending on its place in its orbit. The planet travels a greater distance when it is close to the sun and a smaller distance when it is far from the sun. However, over equal times, the area covered by an imaginary line from the center of the planet to the center of the sun will be equal.

Seasons are *not* determined by Earth's distance from the sun. Earth is at perihelion (closest to the sun) in early January. It is at aphelion (farthest from the sun) in July. What causes the change in seasons is the position (or slant) of Earth in relation to the sun. When the North Pole is slanted toward the sun, the Northern Hemisphere receives more light, and it is spring and summer there. When the North Pole is slanted away from the sun, the Northern Hemisphere receives less light, and it is autumn and winter there.

The equinoxes occur at the two halfway points between Earth's perihelion and aphelion. *Equinox* means "equal night." On the equinoxes, day and night everywhere on Earth are nearly equal. The distance from equinox to equinox is the same along both halves of Earth's elliptical orbit.

Even though the distances are the same, the time it takes Earth to travel the two halves of the ellipse are different. This is because Earth is traveling faster when it is near the sun (in January) and slower when it is farther away (in July). This explains why spring and summer combined are about four days longer than fall and winter on Earth's Northern Hemisphere. The opposite is true for the Southern Hemisphere.

If you lived on Mars you would notice a bigger difference in the length of the seasons. Mars's northern hemisphere has 373 days of spring and summer, but only 276 days of fall and winter.[9] The reason Mars has such a big difference is the flatness of its elliptical orbit.

Snowflakes, Galileo, and Prague

"JUST THEN BY A HAPPY CHANCE . . . SNOW, and specks of down fell here and there on my coat, all with six corners," Kepler wrote. Why, he wondered, did snowflakes all have six sides? "If it happens by chance," he asked, "why do they not fall just as well with five corners or seven?"[1]

Kepler wrote a small, lighthearted book exploring possible causes of a snowflake's shape. The book was called *The Strena*. *The Strena* was a New Year's present for one of his friends in Prague, Johann Matthäus Wackher von Wackenfels.

Wondering about snowflakes was as natural to

Kepler as pondering light, life on other planets, or the volume of wine barrels. Astronomy was his driving goal, but he had many other interests, too. In Prague, he was able to pursue them. Prague was an exciting city with many intellectual people. Kepler found friends there with whom he could discuss astronomy, mathematics, the size of Earth, fountains, snowflakes, and more.

When Rudolph II became emperor in 1576, he chose Prague as his residence. Prague, now the capital of the Czech Republic, was then a part of Bohemia. Bohemia was one of the territories in the Holy Roman Empire. Rudolph brought energy and excitement to the city. Diplomats, scholars, and advisors came to Prague because the emperor was there.[2] The new emperor loved art and music, so artists and musicians flocked there. Rudolph was interested in science, so men with great ideas, like Tycho Brahe and Johannes Kepler, were appointed to his court.

Kepler's achievements in Prague were considerable. The *New Astronomy* became one of the major works of the scientific revolution. However, he also enjoyed other successes. Kepler was curious about light and how light travels. He did many experiments and wrote two important books about optics, the science of light.

In 1600 Kepler observed a solar eclipse. A solar eclipse occurs when the moon passes directly between Earth and the sun, covering up the face of the sun. Tycho had commented to Kepler that in some of his eclipse observations it appeared that the moon did not fully cover the sun.

With directions from Tycho, Kepler made a pinhole camera to watch the eclipse. A pinhole camera is not like a modern camera. It has no lens and uses no film. In Kepler's time, a camera was used for observing, not photography. A pinhole camera can be used to observe the sun because it projects the sun's image on a piece of paper or another surface. With a pinhole camera, the viewer looks at the sun's projected image rather than at the sun itself. It is never safe to look directly at the sun.

Kepler's eclipse observations seemed to show the same results as Tycho's. Kepler wondered if the answer was with the sun, the moon, or the device. He experimented with the size of the pinhole (called the aperture.) He made models with strings to understand how light passes through a tiny aperture. Carrying the thought further, Kepler figured out how light is projected on the human eye.[3] Kepler's book *Astronomia Pars Optica*, which means "the Optical Part of Astronomy," was published in 1604.

One March day in 1610, Wackenfels (Kepler's snowflake friend) arrived at Kepler's house. He was bursting with excitement. Still in his carriage, he shared thrilling news. Galileo Galilei in Italy had turned a telescope to the heavens and seen amazing things. Wackenfels had heard that Galileo had discovered four new planets. Wackenfels and Kepler were so excited they could barely talk.[4]

Kepler doubted that they were actually planets. "Galileo has quite possibly seen four other very tiny moons," he wrote.[5] Galileo's book *Sidereus Nuncius* ("the Starry Messenger") arrived a few weeks later. It announced Galileo's discovery of the moons of Jupiter. The reports that Wackenfels had heard were wrong. Galileo had not discovered planets, but moons, just as Kepler had thought.

Kepler was very excited about Galileo's discoveries and wrote a long letter to him. "Press on vigorously with your observations," Kepler wrote to Galileo, "and let us know at the very earliest opportunity what results your observations have attained."[6]

Kepler was desperate to get a telescope so that he might see these things, too. A few months later, his wish was fulfilled. With the telescope, he saw the moons of Jupiter for himself. Kepler, of course, wanted to know how the telescope worked. He spent weeks studying how light passes through lenses. Then he wrote a book called *Dioptrice* about light and lenses.

In Prague, Kepler returned to a manuscript he had started writing when he was younger. "Fifty thousand German miles up in the ether is the island of Levania," he wrote. "The road to it from here or from it to this earth is seldom

A portrait of Italian astronomer and scientist, Galileo. Kepler corresponded with Galileo about the developments that were taking place in astronomy during their time.

open."[7] In Kepler's story, a young man travels to Levania, the moon. He describes how the residents of one side of the moon always have a view of Earth. Those on the other side never see it. This book would later be called *The Dream*. Kepler did not finish writing it in Prague. He would return to *The Dream* later in his life, but would never fully finish it.

Kepler's years in Prague were creative and productive. As Imperial Mathematician he made friends with noblemen and intellectuals who shared his interests.

Emperor Rudolph II liked Kepler and

supported his work. Rudolph, however, had his own problems in life. Severe depression made him increasingly shy and reclusive. Some people thought Rudolph was insane. As religious and political divisions grew, he made erratic and irresponsible decisions. Kepler stayed close to his emperor through difficult times.

One of Rudolph's faults was that he seldom paid what he owed people. Kepler never collected his full salary. The inheritance of Kepler's wife, Barbara, paid many of their bills.

Barbara Kepler missed her home in Graz and was not happy in Prague. She did not understand Kepler's work and was not interested in learning about it. Prayers were the only things she read. She was apparently more charming to people outside of her home than she was to her husband. Frequent illnesses made her life even more difficult. Her joy in life, other than prayer, was her children.[8] In Prague, the Keplers had two sons and a daughter.

In 1611, the fragile situation in Prague collapsed. So did Kepler's family life.

Rudolph's instability had become obvious to

many nobles. Many felt that Matthias, Rudolph's brother, should become emperor. Soldiers came into Prague and there was fighting in the city. Rudolph was forced out. Matthias was then elected emperor of the Holy Roman Empire.

As the political situation boiled, Barbara Kepler was ill. Then her children all caught smallpox. The middle child, six-year-old Frederick, died. The other two survived. Barbara, who had been recovering, caught a disease called typhus.

"In melancholy despondency, the saddest frame of mind under the sun, she finally expired," Kepler wrote.[9] In five months' time, his wife and son had both died.

Kepler's life was torn apart, and so was Prague. Matthias did not share Rudolph's tolerance for Protestants. Kepler wanted to be in a region more accepting of his Lutheran religion. He needed to care for his two children. He wanted to continue his work in peace.

Brides, Barrels, and Witches

AFTER PRAGUE, KEPLER MADE A NEW home in Linz, an old city in upper Austria. Many Lutherans lived there. Kepler arrived in Linz in an unusual situation. He was still officially Imperial Mathematician and received a small salary from the new emperor, Matthias. He was also the Linz district mathematician. The job had been created for him by a group of Protestant noblemen.[1] In Linz, Kepler hoped to be safe from the turmoil of Prague. The emperor and the noblemen were all looking forward to the *Rudolphine Tables*.

Shortly after arriving in Linz, Kepler went to

the Lutheran church to meet the pastor. As they talked, Kepler revealed some of his personal concerns about his faith. He was especially troubled that two Protestant religions, Lutheranism and Calvinism, were not more accepting of each other. To Kepler, some of the Calvinist beliefs seemed reasonable. The pastor asked Kepler to sign a paper saying he supported all the beliefs of the Lutheran Church. Kepler said he would sign it with one exception. The pastor would not allow any exceptions. He refused to let Kepler belong to the church.[2] Kepler knew the pastor would accept him if he would sign the paper, but he could not go against his true beliefs.

"I have no right to be hypocritical in matters of conscience," he wrote.[3] Religion was profoundly important to Kepler. It was very painful to him to be kept away from his church.

Despite his problems with the church, happiness came into Kepler's life in Linz. When he arrived there, he was a single father with a young daughter and son. He needed a wife. Friends introduced women to him. Altogether, eleven women were suggested as candidates to be his bride. There were rich ones, poor ones, a plump one, and one who was a friend of his first wife.[4] The widower was overwhelmed. As he wavered, a few of these women married other men.

In the end, Kepler married Susanna Reuttinger, a twenty-four-year-old orphan. She lived near Linz and had been raised by a baroness. Susanna had no money but had a good upbringing. They were married in October 1613, in a festive celebration. Emperor Matthias sent them a valuable goblet as a wedding gift.[5] Susanna cared for Kepler's two children, and they had six more. Only two of these six children lived to adulthood, however.

The year of Kepler's second marriage was a good one for Austrian wine. Kepler purchased wine barrels for the family's new home. When the wine dealer made his delivery, he poked a measuring stick into each barrel. The mark on the stick showed the volume of the wine. The dealer used the same stick for different size barrels and did no calculations at all.

Kepler was amazed. He had to see if this method was mathematically accurate. Astronomy was foremost in his mind, but he leapt into the problem of calculating the volume of barrels. Besides barrels, he calculated volumes for cones and spheres and all kinds of shapes with curved sides. He calculated olive shapes, apple shapes, plum shapes, and lemon shapes.[6] The book he wrote about this mathematical exercise is called *Nova Stereometria*. In the history of mathematics, Kepler's barrel work was a step toward the development of a new branch of mathematics called integral calculus. In the end, Kepler's calculations showed that the dealer's measuring rod was accurate.

Kepler lived during a time when many ideas were changing. New inventions and education were transforming Europe. However, it was also a time when many people believed in magic, witches, and superstition.

Many Europeans in Kepler's time believed in witchcraft. Witches supposedly had evil powers and could harm people, animals, or crops with magic spells.[7] The fear of witchcraft was so widespread that it was actually treated as a crime. People suspected of witchcraft were charged in courts of law. If they were found guilty, they were sentenced to severe punishment, often death. Witch hunting in Germany reached its peak during Kepler's time. Estimates are that 100,000 people were killed in Europe as witches in the 1500s and 1600s. The vast majority of them were women.[8]

Katharina Kepler, Johannes's mother, with her restless personality, quarrelsome nature, and herbal brews, fell into the witch hunters' trap.

Frau Kepler's problem began with a woman named Ursula Reinbold. (*Frau* means "Mrs." in German.) The two women knew each other for a long time. One day, in 1615, they quarreled.[9]

After the argument, Ursula Reinbold was furious about the things Katharina Kepler said. Reinbold began to spread rumors and tales about Kepler's mother. Reinbold started telling stories about things that had happened long before their dispute. She told people that once Katharina Kepler served her a drink. Reinbold told them that she fell ill after drinking it. The drink, she said, must have been poisoned. As Frau Reinbold spread her story, other people started remembering things too. The butcher's wife remembered that her husband felt pains in his leg after Katharina Kepler walked by. The schoolmaster said he drank one of her potions and became lame. The tailor said that his two children died after she leaned over their cradle. A woman who worked for Ursula Reinbold claimed to know certain things about witches. She said she could tell if a person had been bewitched by measuring their head. The woman measured Ursula Reinbold's head. Yes, she proclaimed, Reinbold had been bewitched.[10]

Rumors ran wild. In a nasty scene, Ursula Reinbold's brother accused Katharina Kepler of witchcraft. Reinbold's brother pulled out his sword. He touched Katharina Kepler on the chest with it and threatened to kill her if she did not heal his sister.

Katharina Kepler was outraged. She filed a legal complaint against the Reinbolds for their false accusations. Time dragged on before the court would hear her complaint. A date nearly a year later was set for the court hearing.

Eight days before the hearing, as Katharina Kepler was walking down the street one day, she met a group of young girls. One of the girls was the daughter of the woman who had measured Ursula Reinbold's bewitched head. Katharina Kepler brushed against the girls as she passed. She turned to look back at them.[11]

The daughter told a different story. She claimed Katharina Kepler hit her on the arm. Pain, the girl said, crept through her arm until she could not move her hand or fingers.

"It is a witch grip," said a court official when he looked at the girl's arm. He canceled the hearing for Katharina Kepler's complaint against the Reinbolds. He said he had to report the incident with the girls to higher authorities. Katharina Kepler then made the situation worse. She offered him a silver cup if he would have the hearing and not file the report.[12]

Katharina Kepler then left town and went to Linz. She stayed with Johannes Kepler and his wife for several months. When she returned to

Despite the scientific advances that were being made in Kepler's time, much superstition still persisted. Kepler's own mother, Katharina, was accused of being a witch. An accused witch might have been hanged or burned at the stake, as shown in this print from 1555.

her home the following spring, she hoped to finally have her complaint heard in court.

Katharina Kepler never got the hearing to clear her name. Instead, she was charged with witchcraft. On August 7, 1620, Katharina Kepler was arrested in her bed and carried to prison in a closed chest. In court she insisted she was innocent. She vowed that she was not a witch.[13]

German courts handled many witchcraft trials then. Court officials claimed that witches usually said they were innocent. To get confessions, the accused witches were often tortured. Time after time, the accused could not bear the pain of the torture. To make their tormentors stop they would confess. When the accused witch confessed, the court sentenced her. Usually the sentence was death. Burning at the stake was a standard execution, although the condemned were sometimes strangled first.

Katharina Kepler was chained in jail for fourteen months. She expected to be tortured.

Johannes Kepler left Linz and went to his mother's aid. He took over her legal defense. He hired lawyers and wrote long detailed reports.

Finally the court reached its decision. It was long and complicated. The court decided that there was not enough evidence that Katharina Kepler was a witch to authorize her torture. However, they also said that there was not enough evidence to find her innocent. They decided that she should be led to the torture chamber but not actually harmed. If she confessed, then they would sentence her.

Seventy-year-old Katharina Kepler was led to a torture chamber by her jailers. She was shown the torture instruments and asked if she would confess. "Do with me what you want," she said. "Even if you were to pull one vein after another from my body, I would have nothing to admit." She then fell to her knees and prayed.[14]

She was led back to prison and set free. Katharina Kepler was exhausted from her ordeal. She died six months later.

9

Harmony and the Third Law

AS USUAL, KEPLER WAS WORKING ON several projects while he lived in Linz. Through his mother's trial, he continued his search for the plan of the universe. Three major projects filled his days: the *Rudolphine Tables*, a series of textbooks, and his favorite, the *Harmonice Mundi*.

The *Rudolphine Tables* hung over him for years. His "war with Mars" had paved the way for his work on the other planets. The tables, though, still required much toil. Kepler needed to calculate the elliptical orbit of each planet and the moon. Kepler was still owed much money by the emperor. He could not afford to hire an assistant and had to do most of the computing himself.

"I beg you my friends not to condemn me entirely to the treadmill of mathematical calculations," Kepler wrote when his employers urged him to hurry his work on the tables. "Leave me some time for philosophical speculations, which are my only delight," he begged.[1] Kepler finished most of the calculations of the planets by the end of 1616. The moon, however, posed some different challenges. Kepler could not finish the tables without resolving the moon's movement.

Another project also consumed Kepler's time in Linz. He was writing a series of textbooks on Copernicus's astronomy. Written with straightforward questions and answers, he wanted the books to be easy to understand. They would explain the working of the sun-centered solar system. Kepler named the project *Epitome Astronomia Copernicanae*. The title translates to "A Compendium of Copernican Astronomy." In fact, Kepler's discoveries vastly changed Copernicus's model. Epicycles and circles were gone. Elliptical orbits with great distances between them now explained the solar system. Copernicus's sun-centered plan had been enormously improved by Kepler.

During this time, tragedy again struck Kepler's family. One of his young daughters died. Kepler found it hard to keep his mind on his work. It was especially hard to do the tedious calculations required for the *Rudolphine Tables*.

"I set the Tables aside since they required peace," he wrote, "and turned my mind to the contemplation of the Harmony."[2] In February 1618, he returned to a project he had thought about for more than twenty years.

From the time he first wrote *Mysterium Cosmographicum*, Kepler had planned his *Harmonice Mundi*. *Harmonice Mundi* translates roughly to "Harmony of the World." The *Harmonice* was Kepler's vision of the universe. It was a grand vision. From the beginning, Kepler had believed that there was a plan for the universe. He believed that there was mathematical beauty in the universe similar to that found in music.

In music, there are mathematical relationships between different notes. Think of the strings of a harp. Each string of the harp produces a different sound when plucked. This is because each string has a specific length and there is a mathematical proportion between their lengths. Each string is a precise amount shorter or longer than the strings next to it.

The relationships between these lengths accounts for the pleasing sound of different combinations of notes. This is called harmony.

Kepler believed that there was a similar harmony in the universe. To find it he looked for relationships between the distances and speed of the planets. From the time he wrote *Mysterium Cosmographicum* he knew that planets more distant from the sun moved faster than those close to it. He believed a force from the sun drove the planets. However, from the beginning, he suspected that there was no easy answer to explain the relationship between the planets' speeds and their distances from the sun. He wrote in *Mysterium Cosmographicum*, "you will discover that there is no room for a simple proportion [to describe it]."[3]

On May 15, 1618, Kepler made a thrilling discovery. He was exuberant. "A most remarkable spectacle has risen," he wrote. "Nothing holds me back. I give myself up to sacred frenzy. . . . If you pardon me, I am happy."[4]

Kepler had discovered his third law of planetary motion. The law showed that the amount of time it takes a planet to orbit the sun is related to its distance from the sun. Kepler discovered the mathematical proportion that explained this relationship. Like Kepler's second law of planetary motion, mathematical calculations are needed to apply the third law. He had been right that it was not a simple answer.

Kepler's third law of planetary motion is often expressed as follows: "The square of the orbital period [time for a complete orbit] of a planet around the sun is proportional to the cube of the planet's average distance from the sun."[5]

The law means that planets move in a predictable way depending on their distance from the sun. Understanding the terms Kepler uses makes it easier to understand this relationship. To *square* a number means to multiply a number by itself. Two times two is four. You could also say two *squared* equals four. Four is the *square* of two. To *cube* a number means to multiply a number by itself three times. Two times two times two is eight. Two *cubed* is eight. Eight is the *cube* of two.

With Kepler's third law he could finally calculate the relative distances of the planets' orbits from each other and from the sun. Relative distance means how the distances are related to each other. Kepler did not know the planets' distances in miles or kilometers from the sun. Instead, he could figure out how much closer or more distant each one was compared to the others. Kepler could see that Jupiter was a little more than five times as far from the sun as Earth. He could calculate that Venus was about three quarters as far from the sun as Earth. He finally had a true picture of the distances between the planets.

Kepler's third law of planetary motion does much more than just explain these relative distances.

Think about objects orbiting Earth. The International Space Station orbits Earth approximately every 92 minutes. It has a very short orbital period. Some communications satellites are in orbits that keep them over the same point on Earth all the time. Are they orbiting Earth? Yes, their orbital period is the same as one rotation of Earth, about 24 hours. This is called *geostationary* orbit.

Which one must be farther from Earth? The geostationary satellite must be higher. It orbits at about 22,000 miles above Earth. It could not orbit so slowly any closer to Earth. Gravity would pull it down. The International Space Station orbits at about 220 miles above Earth. It can orbit lower because it is traveling so fast—17,500 miles per hour.

Knowledge of Kepler's third law of planetary

motion opened up understanding of many more things in space. This law actually describes the relationship between the masses of two objects revolving around each other. What Kepler discovered about the sun and planets can be adjusted to deal with stars that are larger and smaller than our sun. The law can be used with planets and their moons.

Today scientists study other stars looking for other planetary systems. One thing they look for is a "wobble" in the movement of stars. That "wobble" means that another mass is orbiting around it. Gravity from each of the two masses, the star and its planet, is pulling on the other. Even though we cannot see the planet, we can learn about it by applying Kepler's third law of planetary motion.

In 2006 NASA will launch the Kepler Mission. The purpose of this space mission is to detect Earth-sized planets around other stars in our galaxy. The mission will be looking for planets that may be similar to Earth. The mission will use Kepler's third law in its search.

Final Years

KEPLER HOPED TO HAVE PEACE TO FINISH the *Rudolphine Tables*. That possibility vanished exactly eight days after he discovered his third law of planetary motion.

On May 23, 1618, a group of Protestant noblemen marched into the castle in Prague. The noblemen picked up two Catholic officials and threw them out the window. This "defenestration of Prague," signaled the beginning of the Thirty Years' War. Accounts of the event claim that the officials survived because a dung-heap beneath the window cushioned their fall.[1] The revolt, however, had started. Many Protestant nobles would no longer accept Catholic rule. Bloody battles would be waged across Europe as religious and political groups struggled for power. The Thirty Years' War tore the Holy Roman Empire into pieces.

Although the war did not immediately come to Linz, unrest grew. Even in this tense atmosphere, Kepler kept working.

In 1621, the final volumes of his textbooks, the *Epitome Astronomia Copernicanae*, were complete. These were among the most widely read astronomy books in Europe between 1630 and 1650.[2] In them, with questions and answers, Kepler carefully explained the sun-centered universe. The laws of planetary motion that he had discovered were all presented in them. These straightforward textbooks were easier for most readers to understand than many of Kepler's other works. They played an important part in changing European ideas about the universe.

In Linz, Kepler also wrote and published a short book about comets. He published a second edition of *Mysterium Cosmographicum*, the work with which he started his search. This edition included detailed notes. They explained his many discoveries and further investigation of the harmony of the universe. He published a mathematics book and ephemerides. (Ephemerides are lists of the positions of planets at different times.)

Kepler untangled his final problems with the moon and completed the *Rudolphine Tables*. The years of calculations were over. Only the task of publishing them remained. However, it was a big task. Thirty-five years of Tycho's observations and twenty-five years of Kepler's calculations went into this work. For the tables to be useful, the publishing had to be flawless.

Kepler still had not been fully paid for his years as Rudolph's Imperial Mathematician. He was owed more than 6,300 gulden, an enormous sum of money at the time. To discuss the tables and his overdue payment, Kepler visited the new emperor, Ferdinand II. Ferdinand was co-operative, but Kepler only collected about a third of what he was owed.[3]

In 1626, Johannes Plank, the local printer in

Linz, was prepared to start printing the *Rudolphine Tables*. Suddenly, everything changed. It was as though Kepler were back in Graz. The Catholic prince was tightening his hold on his territory. All the Protestant "preachers and un-Catholic schoolmasters" were expelled.[4] Everyone who stayed in the city must attend Catholic mass. Anyone who did not was banished. Kepler was given an exception. He and his family could stay, but his children had to attend the Catholic church. This time, he agreed.

In the region around Linz, Protestant peasants felt that they had suffered enough. They organized into armies and attacked Catholic property and people. They burned churches and castles. They set siege to Linz. Food and supplies could not come into the city. Hunger and disease spread, but the residents could not leave. The peasants set fire to houses that were outside the city wall. One of the burned houses belonged to Johannes Plank. Plank's printing press went up in flames.[5]

Catholic armies defeated the peasants and

the siege ended. Kepler left Linz with his family and the manuscript for the *Rudolphine Tables*.

Kepler spent most of 1627 supervising the publishing of the *Rudolphine Tables* in the city of Ulm. What joy he must have felt at seeing this great work complete at last!

One thousand copies of the *Rudolphine Tables* were printed in the first edition. It was a large volume printed on fine quality paper. The title page announced The *Rudolphine Tables*, by Tycho Brahe, for the Emperors Rudolph, Matthias, and Ferdinand. Johannes Kepler is listed below, as assistant to the project. Kepler always honored Tycho's legacy. Tycho's superb observations were the building blocks with which Kepler built a new, more accurate, sun-centered model of the solar system.

The *Rudolphine Tables* were a major astronomical work. They provided the information needed to calculate the positions of the planets and moon for any time in the past or future.[6] In addition to the planetary information, the tables included Tycho's catalogue of 1,000 stars.

Using Kepler's tables, astronomers could

TABULÆ

RUDOLPHINÆ,

QUIBUS ASTRONOMICÆ SCIENTIÆ, TEMPO-
rum longinquitate collapsæ RESTAURATIO continetur;

A Phœnice illo Aſtronomorum

TYCHONE,

Ex Illuſtri & Generoſa BRAHEORUM in Regno Daniæ
familiâ oriundo Equite,

PRIMUM ANIMO CONCEPTA ET DESTINA-
TA ANNO CHRISTI MDLXIV: EXINDE OBSERVATIONIBUS
SIDERUM ACCURATISSIMIS, POST ANNUM PRÆCIPUE MDLXXII,
Quo SIDUS IN CASSIOPEIÆ CONSTELLATIONE NOVUM EFFULSIT · SERIÒ AFFECTATA; VARIIS
que operibus, cùm mechanicis, tùm librariis, impenſo patrimonio ampliſſimo, accedentibus etiam ſubſidiis FRI-
DERICI II. DANIÆ REGIS, regali magnificentiâ dignis, tracta per annos XXV. potiſſimùm in Inſula
freti SUNDICI HUENNA, &arce URANIBURGO, in hos uſus à fun-
damentis extructâ:

TANDEM TRADUCTA IN GERMANIAM, INQUE AULAM ET
Nomen RUDOLPHI IMP. anno MDIIC.

TABULAS IPSAS, JAM ET NUNCUPATAS, ET AFFECTAS, SED
MORTE AUTHORIS SUI ANNO MDCI. DESERTAS,

JUSSU ET STIPENDIIS FRETUS TRIUM IMPPP.

RUDOLPHI, MATTHIÆ, FERDINANDI,

ANNITENTIBUS HÆREDIBUS BRAHEANIS; EX FUNDAMENTIS OB-
ſervationum relictarum: ad exemplum ferè partim jam exſtructarum; continuis multorum annorum ſpe-
culationibus, & computationibus, primùm PRAGÆ Bohemorum continuavit; deinde LINCII,
Superioris Auſtriæ Metropoli, ſubſidiis etiam Ill. Provincialium adjutus, perfecit, ab-
ſolvit: adq; cauſarum & calculi perennis formulam traduxit.

IOANNES KEPLERUS,

TYCHONI primùm à RUDOLPHO II. Imp. adjunctus calculi miniſter; indéq;
Trium ordine Imppp. Mathematicus:

Qui idem de ſpeciali mandato FERDINANDI II. IMP.
petentibus inſtantibúsq; Hæredibus,

Opus hoc ad uſus præſentium & poſteritatis, typis, numericis propriis, cæteris, & prælo
JONÆ SAURII, Reip. Ulmanæ Typographi, in publicum extulit, &
Typographicis operis ULMÆ curator affuit.

Cum Privilegiis, IMP. & RegumRerúmq; publ. vivo TYCHONI ejúsq; Hæredibus,
& ſpeciali Imperatorio, ipſi KEPLERO conceſſo, ad Annos XXX.

ANNO M. D C. XXVII.

The Rudolphine Tables were begun by Tycho Brahe using his vast collection of observations. The tables were finally completed by Johannes Kepler and published in 1627.

calculate when eclipses would occur. They knew when Venus would be a morning star or an evening star. They could predict conjunctions, (when two planets are lined up in the sky). With the *Rudolphine Tables*, they knew when Mercury would pass across the face of the sun. As a result of the *Rudolphine Tables*, predictions of planetary movement were 100 times more accurate than before.

The *Rudolphine Tables* were Kepler's last major astronomical project. He continued writing his science fiction story, *The Dream*. He wrote more ephemerides (planet lists) that were based on his tables. He also planned to publish more of Tycho's observations.

As war tore through the Empire, it was hard to find peace. It was even harder to find a home where Protestants were tolerated. Kepler was still short of money. Altogether he was owed more than 12,000 gulden. In November 1630, he was returning home from another attempt to collect his money. He stopped in the city of Regensburg where he had friends. While there, he fell ill with

This monument was erected in honor of Kepler in Regensburg, the city where he died in 1630. The monument is near the location of the cemetery where Kepler was buried. The cemetery was destroyed in 1634, during the Thirty Years' War.

a blazing fever. Johannes Kepler died on November 15, 1630.

Kepler had composed an epitaph to be on his grave. In English it reads:

"I used to measure the heavens, now I shall measure the shadows of Earth. Although my soul was from heaven, the shadow of my body lies here."[7]

In the chaos of the Thirty Years' War, the Protestant cemetery where he was buried was destroyed.

Johannes Kepler changed the science of the heavens. Attracted by Copernicus's heliocentric theory, Kepler set out on a quest to learn the plan of the universe. When he started, the model of the universe was clumsy and inaccurate. Circles on top of circles were believed to spin on crystal spheres.

With Copernicus's sun-centered model and Tycho's observations, Kepler built a truly new astronomy. His vision of mathematical explanations and his demand for causes yielded answers. As a result of his discoveries, people could see that planets moved in a predictable

Bust of Kepler that stands in the Regensburg Monument.

way along elliptical paths through space. Natural laws explained their motion. People might not have wanted to change their view of the universe, but it was hard to ignore the fact that the *Rudolphine Tables* worked. With their stunning accuracy, the *Rudolphine Tables* proved the truth of the Copernican system as refined by Kepler.

Activities

Activity One: Pinhole Projector

On July 10, 1600, Johannes Kepler observed a solar eclipse using a pinhole camera. A solar eclipse occurs when the moon passes directly between the sun and Earth. At least two and no more than five solar eclipses are visible from Earth each year. However, each eclipse is only visible in the small area that falls under the moon's shadow.

A device similar to the one Kepler used is a safe way to observe an eclipse. **It is never safe to look directly at the sun.**

You need two pieces of cardboard, one of which must be white. The white cardboard will be the screen on which the sun's image is projected. Poke a tiny hole through the middle of the other piece of cardboard. Line up the two pieces so that the sun's rays pass through the hole and are projected on the white cardboard. By setting the white cardboard on the ground, you can move the cardboard with the pinhole into position. During the eclipse, watch the white cardboard to see the moon move across the sun.

The greater the distance between the two pieces of cardboard, the larger the image. The image of the sun will be approximately 1/100 the distance between your two pieces of cardboard.

As you watch the eclipse, you will notice something else. The image of the eclipse will be reversed. This is because the light travels in straight lines. The light rays do not bend as they pass through the tiny aperture. The light rays that enter from the right go in a straight line to the left. Those coming from the left pass through and are seen on the right.

Activity Two: Observing Planetary Motion

The word *planet* comes from the Greek word for "wanderer." The planets' apparent wandering through the heavens perplexed people for many centuries. Kepler's discoveries explained the movement of the planets.

When you look at the sky on just one night, you do not see the planets moving against the background stars. If you observe them for several nights, you will begin to see their wandering.

You will need:

    Paper and pencil

    At least three clear nights

    The position of Venus

Venus is the third brightest celestial object viewed from Earth. Only the sun and moon are brighter. Venus is closer to the sun than is Earth. Therefore it is never seen on the opposite side of Earth from the sun. You will not see Venus in the middle of the night. Depending on where Venus is in its orbit, it is visible from Earth either in the early morning, before the sun rises, or in the evening after the sun sets.

You can learn about Venus from various web sites, including www.skymaps.com or from your newspaper. Many newspapers list information about the planets with the weather.

On a clear night go outdoors to observe Venus. Once you have identified Venus, carefully observe the brightest stars near it. Draw a diagram showing those stars. You can use your hand as a tool to measure the observed distances between the stars. Some of the stars may be a thumb-width or a pinky-length apart. After you have drawn the stars, carefully mark Venus's position. Label it "A" on your sketch. On the side of the paper, label "A" with the date.

After a few days, go back outside at about the same time of night. Find Venus again and mark its position on your diagram. Label this point "B," and note the date. Go out at least one more time to observe and record Venus's position again. Which way has Venus moved against the background stars?

Activity Three: Drawing Ellipses

Through his "war with Mars," Kepler discovered that planets follow elliptical paths. Kepler's first law of planetary motion is often stated this way: Each planet revolves around the sun in an elliptical path, with the sun occupying one focus of the ellipse.

This discovery revealed that the planets do not follow perfectly circular orbits.

To draw ellipses, you will need:
> String
> Two pushpins
> A piece of cardboard
> A pencil or pen

Tie the string into a loop. Put the two pins into the cardboard far enough apart that the string is quite loose. Use your pencil to pull the string tight. Carefully keeping the loop of string tight, move your pencil around the tacks. When your pencil arrives back at the point where it started, you have drawn your ellipse.

Now, move one of the pins and push it back into the cardboard. It may be closer or farther from the first pin. Draw another ellipse. This ellipse will be flatter if the distance between the two pins is greater than it was when you drew the first ellipse. If the pins are closer together, then the ellipse will be rounder. The flatness or

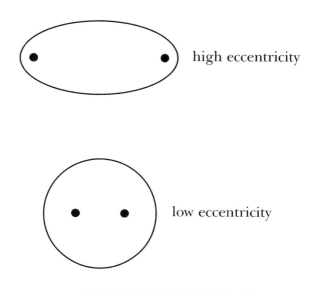

high eccentricity

low eccentricity

Examples of a low-eccentrcity ellipse and a high-eccentrcity ellipse.

roundness of the ellipse is its eccentricity. A flatter ellipse has greater eccentricity than a rounder ellipse.

You may draw ellipses with longer and shorter pieces of string. Leave one pin in the same position as you draw your different ellipses. This will give you an idea of how the sun can be at one focus of many different elliptical orbits.

Chronology

1571—December 27: Johannes Kepler is born in Weil der Stadt (now in southern Germany).

1576—Kepler family moves to Leonberg.

1577—Observes Great Comet of 1577 with his mother, Katharina Kepler.

1579—Enrolls in Latin School in Leonberg.

1584—Enters Adelberg monastery school, the beginning of religious training.

1589—Begins five-year theology program at University of Tübingen.

1594—Arrives in Graz, Austria, to be mathematics and astronomy teacher.

1596—Writes *Mysterium Cosmographicum* ("Secret of the Universe"). The book is published the following year.

1597—Marries Barbara Müller.

1598—Protestant teachers and preachers banished from Graz.

1599—Outlines books on *Harmonice Mundi* ("Harmony of the World").

1600—Meets Tycho Brahe at Benatky Castle near Prague. Begins calculations to determine the path of Mars. Returns briefly to Graz. Observes solar eclipse with a pinhole camera on July 10. Non-Catholics banished from Graz. With his wife and stepdaughter, goes to work with Tycho Brahe in Prague.

1601—Tycho Brahe announces *Rudolphine Tables* to be written with Kepler.

October 24: Tycho Brahe dies. Kepler appointed Imperial Mathematician.

1604—Publishes *Astronomiae Pars Optica*, a book about optics and astronomy.

1605—Discovers elliptical path of Mars. Discovery leads to first law of planetary motion. Finishes writing *Astronomia Nova* ("The New Astronomy"), which includes his second law of planetary motion.

1609—*Astronomia Nova* is published.

1610—Receives *Sidereus Nuncius* ("Starry Messenger") from Galileo. Uses telescope and observes moons of Jupiter.

1611—Publishes *Dioptrice*, a book on optics. Publishes *The Strena*, a book about snowflakes. Wife and son die.

1612—Moves to Linz in Austria. Excluded from Lutheran church there.

1613—Marries Susanna Reuttinger.

1615—Publishes *Nova Stereometria*, a book on mathematical calculation of the volume of wine barrels and other objects with curved sides.

1615–1621—Katharina Kepler's witchcraft charge and trial.

1617–1622—Publishes *Epitome Astronomiae Copernicanae* (textbooks about Copernican, sun-centered astronomy).

1618–1621—Writes *Harmonice Mundi* ("The Harmony of the World"), which is published the following year. Discovers third law of planetary motion. Thirty Years' War begins with "defenestration of Prague."

1625—Non-Catholics banished from Linz. Siege of Linz.

1626—Leaves Linz.

1627—*Rudolphine Tables* published.

1630—*November 15*: Dies in Regensburg.

Chapter Notes

Chapter 1. The Plan of the Universe

1. Max Caspar, *Kepler,* ed. and trans. C. Doris Hellman (New York: Dover Publications, Inc., 1993), p. 199.

2. Carola Baumgardt, *Johannes Kepler: Life and Letters* (New York: Philosophical Library, 1951), p. 35.

3. Charles Coulston Gillispie, *Dictionary of Scientific Biography* (New York: Scribners, 1973), vol. 7, p. 289.

Chapter 2. Childhood

1. Max Caspar, *Keple,* ed. and trans. C. Doris Hellman (New York: Dover Publications, Inc., 1993), p. 33.

2. Steven Ozment, "Reformation," *World Book* (Chicago: World Book, Inc., 1999).

3. Ibid.

4. Charles Coulston Gillispie, *Dictionary of Scientific Biography* (New York: Scribners, 1973), vol. 7, p. 289.

5. Ibid.

6. Ibid.

7. Caspar, p. 34.

8. Ibid., p. 36.

9. Gillispie, p. 289.

10. Caspar, p. 36.

11. Ibid.

12. Ibid., p. 35.

13. Ibid., p. 37.

14. Ibid., p. 38.

Chapter 3. Discovering Copernicus

1. Max Caspar, *Kepler,* ed. and trans. C. Doris Hellman (New York: Dover Publications, Inc., 1993), p. 44.

2. Charles Coulston Gillispie, *Dictionary of Scientific Biography* (New York: Scribners, 1973) vol. 7, p. 289.

3. Caspar, p. 40.

4. Ibid., p. 52.

5. Ibid., p. 43.

6. Johannes Kepler, *Mysterium Cosmographicum: The Secret of the Universe,* trans. A. M. Duncan (New York: Abaris Books, 1981), p. 63.

7. Ibid.

Chapter 4. Solids and Spheres

1. Max Caspar, *Kepler,* ed. and trans. C. Doris Hellman (New York: Dover Publications, Inc., 1993), p. 56.

2. Ibid., p. 58.

3. Carola Baumgardt, *Johannes Kepler: Life and Letters* (New York: Philosophical Library, 1951), p. 27.

4. Charles Coulston Gillispie, *Dictionary of Scientific Biography* (New York: Scribners, 1973), vol. 7, p. 290.

5. Caspar, p. 60.

6. Johannes Kepler, *Mysterium Cosmographicum: The Secret of the Universe,* trans. A. M. Duncan (New York: Abaris Books, 1981), p. 63.

7. Ibid.

8. Ibid., p. 67.

9. Ibid., p. 63.

10. Gillispie, p. 291.

11. Kepler, *Mysterium Cosmographicum: The Secret of the Universe,* p. 69.

12. Arthur Koestler, *The Sleepwalkers: A History of Man's Changing Vision of the Universe* (London: Arkana, 1959), p. 250.

13. Ibid., p. 271.

14. Caspar, p. 72.

Chapter 5. Turmoil and Tycho

1. Tycho Brahe, "Preface by Tycho Brahe to the Noblest Emperor Rudolph the 2nd," trans. Petr Hadrava, January 1, 1598, <http://www.asu.cas.cz/~had/tychpref.html> (October 15, 2002).

2. Tycho Brahe, *Tycho Brahe's Description of His Instruments and Scientific Work as given in Astronomiae instauratae mechanica, Wandesburgi, 1598,* trans. and ed. Hans Raeder, Elis Stromgren, and Bengt Stromgren (Kobenhavn: Det Kongelige Danske Videnskabernes Selskab, 1946), p. 110.

3. Charles Coulston Gillispie, *Dictionary of Scientific Biography* (New York: Scribners, 1973), vol. 7, p. 293.

4. Max Caspar, *Kepler,* ed. and trans. C. Doris Hellman (New York: Dover Publications, Inc., 1993), p. 70.

5. Edward Rosen, *Three Imperial Mathematicians: Kepler Trapped Between Tycho Brahe and Ursus* (New York: Abaris Books, 1986), p. 110.

6. Caspar, p. 78.

7. Ibid.

8. Ibid.

9. Ibid., p. 79.

10. Johannes Kepler, *The Harmony of the World.* trans. E. J. Aiton, A. M. Duncan, and J. V. Field (Philadelphia: American Philosophical Society, 1997), p. xvi.

11. Caspar, p. 97.

12. Ibid., p. 100.

13. Victor E. Thoren, *The Lord of Uraniborg: A Biography of Tycho Brahe* (Cambridge: Cambridge University Press, 1990), pp. 430–431.

14. Gillispie, p. 307.

15. Caspar, p. 114.

16. John Robert Christianson, *On Tycho's Island: Tycho Brahe and His Assistants 1570–1601* (Cambridge: Cambridge University Press, 2000), p. 303.

Chapter 6. Two Laws of Planetary Motion

1. Johannes Kepler, *New Astronomy* trans. William M. Donahue (Cambridge: Cambridge University Press, 1992), p. 36.

2. Johannes Kepler, *Mysterium Cosmographicum: The Secret of the Universe*, trans. A. M. Duncan (New York: Abaris Books, 1981), p. 212.

3. Arthur Koestler, *The Sleepwalkers: A History of Man's Changing Vision of the Universe* (London: Arkana, 1959), p. 259.

4. Brian Tung, "Music of the Ellipses," *Astronomical Games*, June 2001, <http://astro.isi.edu/games/kepler.html> (August 15, 2002).

5. Kepler, *New Astronomy*, p. 576.

6. Nathan Spielberg and Bryon Anderson, *Seven Ideas That Shook the Universe* (New York: John Wiley & Sons, 1987), p. 45.

7. Ibid.

8. Ibid.

9. Dona Boccio, "Developing a Model of Atmospheric Pressure on Mars: Connecting Concepts in Physics and Mathematics," *Queensborough Community College*, Bayside New York, n.d., <www.amatyc/Proceedings/Pittsburgh25/mars_proceedings.pdf> (August 15, 2002).

Chapter 7. Snowflakes, Galileo, and Prague

1. Johannes Kepler, *The Six-Cornered Snowflake* trans. Colin Hardie (Oxford: Clarendon Press, 1966), p. 7.

2. Max Caspar, *Kepler,* ed. and trans. C. Doris Hellman (New York: Dover Publications, Inc., 1993), p. 151.

3. Ibid., p. 145.

4. Johannes Kepler, *Kepler's Conversation with Galileo's Sidereal Messenger,* trans. Edward Rosen (New York: Johnson Reprint Corp., 1965) p. 10.

5. Ibid.

6. Ibid., p. 48.

7. Johannes Kepler, *Kepler's Somnium: The Dream or Posthumous Work on Lunar Astronomy,* trans. Edward Rosen (Madison: University of Wisconsin Press, 1967), p. 15.

8. Caspar, p. 176.

9. Ibid., p. 207.

Chapter 8. Brides, Barrels, and Witches

1. Max Caspar, *Kepler,* ed. and trans. C. Doris Hellman (New York: Dover Publications, Inc., 1993), p. 212.

2. Ibid., p. 215.

3. Ibid., p. 219.

4. Ibid., p. 222.

5. Ibid.

6. Ibid., p. 234.

7. Geoffrey Scarr, *Witchcraft and Magic in 16th and 17th Century Europe* (Atlantic Highlands, N.J.: Humanities Press International, 1987), p. 3.

8. Ibid., p. 24.

9. Caspar, p. 241.

10. Ibid., p. 243.

11. Ibid., p. 246.

12. Ibid.

13. Ibid., p. 250.

14. Ibid., p. 255.

Chapter 9. Harmony and the Third Law

1. Charles Coulston Gillispie, *Dictionary of Scientific Biography* (New York: Scribners, 1973), vol. 7, p. 300.

2. Max Caspar, *Kepler,* ed. and trans. C. Doris Hellman (New York: Dover Publications, Inc., 1993), p. 265.

3. Johannes Kepler, *Mysterium Cosmographicum: The Secret of the Universe,* trans. A. M. Duncan (New York: Abaris Books, 1981), p. 197.

4. Caspar, p. 267.

5. Nathan Spielberg and Bryon Anderson, *Seven Ideas That Shook the Universe* (New York: John Wiley & Sons, 1987), p. 46.

Chapter 10. Final Years

1. Martin Kitchen, *Germany* (Cambridge: Cambridge University Press, 1966), p. 111.

2. Charles Coulston Gillispie, *Dictionary of Scientific Biography* (New York: Scribners, 1973), vol. 7, p. 302.

3. Max Caspar, *Kepler,* ed. and trans. C. Doris Hellman (New York: Dover Publications, Inc., 1993), p. 315.

4. Ibid., p. 316.

5. Ibid., p. 319.

6. Gillispie, p. 304.

7. Caspar, p. 353.

Glossary

aphelion—The farthest point from the sun in the orbit of a planet, comet, or satellite that revolves around the sun.

astrology—The study of the supposed influence of heavenly bodies on happenings on Earth.

burgher—A free man or citizen of a city. In Kepler's time, usually a member of the merchant class.

clergy—People ordained for religious service.

defenestration—The throwing of a person or a thing out a window.

eccentricity—The roundness or flatness of an ellipse.

ellipse—A geometric shape that looks like a flattened circle.

equinox—The point where the sun's path crosses the celestial equator causing day and night to be exactly equal in all parts of Earth.

Frau—German title, similar to Mrs., for a married woman.

Holy Roman Empire—The empire made up of mostly German and Italian territories that dominated central Europe from approximately 962 to 1806.

horoscope—Diagram of the positions of the planets and stars at a specific point in time used by astrologers to forecast events.

imperial free city—A city in the Holy Roman Empire that was not part of the surrounding territory.

lunar eclipse—The celestial event when Earth passes between the sun and the moon and Earth's shadow passes across the face of the moon.

Lutheran—The Protestant Church founded by Martin Luther.

magistrate—A court official or person empowered to enforce the law.

optics—The study of the properties of light.

perihelion—The nearest point to the sun in the orbit of a planet, comet, or satellite that revolves around the sun.

pinhole camera—An optical observation device. A pinhole camera does not necessarily take photographs.

Reformation—Religious and political movement away from the Roman Catholic Church in Europe in the sixteenth century.

Renaissance—Period from the fourteenth to the seventeenth centuries marked by the revival of classical influence, flowering of arts and literature, and beginning of modern science.

retrograde motion—The apparent backward movement of the planets against the background stars.

solar eclipse—The celestial event when the moon passes in front of the sun as seen from Earth.

tetrahedron—A solid figure with four triangular faces.

Württemberg—Territory in southern Germany that was controlled by the dukes of Württemberg in Kepler's time.

Further Reading

Books

Andronik, Catherine M. *Copernicus: Founder of Modern Astronomy.* Berkeley Heights, N.J.: Enslow Publishers, Inc., 2002.

Gow, Mary. *Tycho Brahe: Astronomer.* Berkeley Heights, N.J.: Enslow Publishers, Inc., 2002.

MacDonald, Fiona. *Space.* Danbury, Conn.: Franklin Watts, Inc., 2000.

Voelkel, James R. *Johannes Kepler & the New Astronomy.* New York: Oxford University Press, Inc., 1999.

Internet Addresses

Johannes Kepler: The Laws of Planetary Motion
http://csep10.phys.utk.edu/astr161/lect/history/kepler.html

Kepler's Laws with Animation
http://home.cvc.org/science/kepler.htm

Kepler's Three Laws of Planetary Motion
http://observe.arc.nasa.gov/nasa/education/reference/orbits/orbit_sim.html

The Golden Age of Astronomy in Prague
http://otokar.troja.mff.cuni.cz/RELATGRP/Rudolf.htm

Index

A

Adelberg, 24
Almagest, 30
aphelion and periphelion, 71
Aristarchus, 32
Aristotle, 28
astrology, 20, 37–38
Astronomia Nova, 65, 74

B

Benatky Castle, 55, 56
Brahe, Tycho, 23, 46, 49–51,
    55–59, 101, 103

C

Charles V, Emperor, 13
Copernicus, Nicolaus, 27, 32,
    34, 38, 66

D

Dream, The, 78, 105

E

ellipse, 64–67, 112–114
epicycles, 30
*Epitome Astronomiae
    Copernicanae*, 92, 100
equinox, 71

F

Ferdinand, Prince, 37, 52
Frederick (King of Denmark),
    50

G

Galilei, Galileo, 12, 46,
    76–77

geometry, 41
Great Comet of 1577, 23

H

Harmonice Mundi, (Harmony
    of the World), 54, 91,
    93
Holy Roman Empire, 8, 14,
    51, 59, 74, 100
horoscope, 20

I

International Space Station,
    5–6, 11, 97

K

Kepler, Heinrich (father), 14,
    18, 20, 21, 22, 24
Kepler, Johannes
    battles Mars, 60–64
    childhood of, 18–24
    death of, 107
    education of, 21–22, 24,
        25–27, 34–35
    Imperial mathematician,
        59, 78–79, 81, 101
    legacy, 107–108
    life in Prague, 74, 76–78
    religious excommunication
        in Linz, 81–82
    religious oppression in
        Graz, 52–55, 58
    religious oppression in
        Linz, 102–103

research on optics, 12,
74–76, 77
teaching career of, 36–38
Kepler, Katharina (mother),
14, 18, 21, 22, 23
witchcraft trial of, 85–90
Kepler Mission, 98
Kepler, Sebald (grandfather),
14, 20
Kepler's Laws of Planetary
Motion
First, 10, 65–67,
Second, 11, 69–70
Third, 11, 95–98

L

Latin schools, 22
Leonberg, 21
lunar eclipse, 24
Luther, Martin, 16–17
Lutherans, 17–18, 36, 81

M

Mastlin, Michael, 26–27, 34,
45
Muller, Barbara (first wife),
48, 54, 58, 79–80
Mysterium Cosmographicum,
45–48, 50, 51, 93, 94,
100

N

Nova Stereometria, 84

O

*On the Revolutions of the
Heavenly Spheres*, 32
orbital period, 62

P

Peace of Augsburg, 18

perfect solids, 43–44
pinhole camera, 75, 109–110
Protestants, 17, 52–53,
99–100, 102, 105
Protestant school in Graz, 35,
36
Ptolemy, 30–32, 66

R

Renaissance, 16
retrograde motion, 30, 66
Reuttinger, Susanna (second
wife), 83
Rudolph II (Emperor of the
Holy Roman Empire),
59, 78–80
Rudolphine Tables, 59, 60, 81,
91, 93, 99, 103, 105,
108

S

smallpox, 21
solar eclipse, 75, 109–110
Strena, The, 73

T

telescope, 76
Tübingen, University of,
25–26, 35, 55

U

Uraniborg, 50

W

Wackenfels, Johann Matthaus
Wacker von, 73, 76–77
Weil der Stadt, 13, 14–16, 18,
21
Württemberg, dukes of, 18,
46